Old Geezers Can Learn to Ski

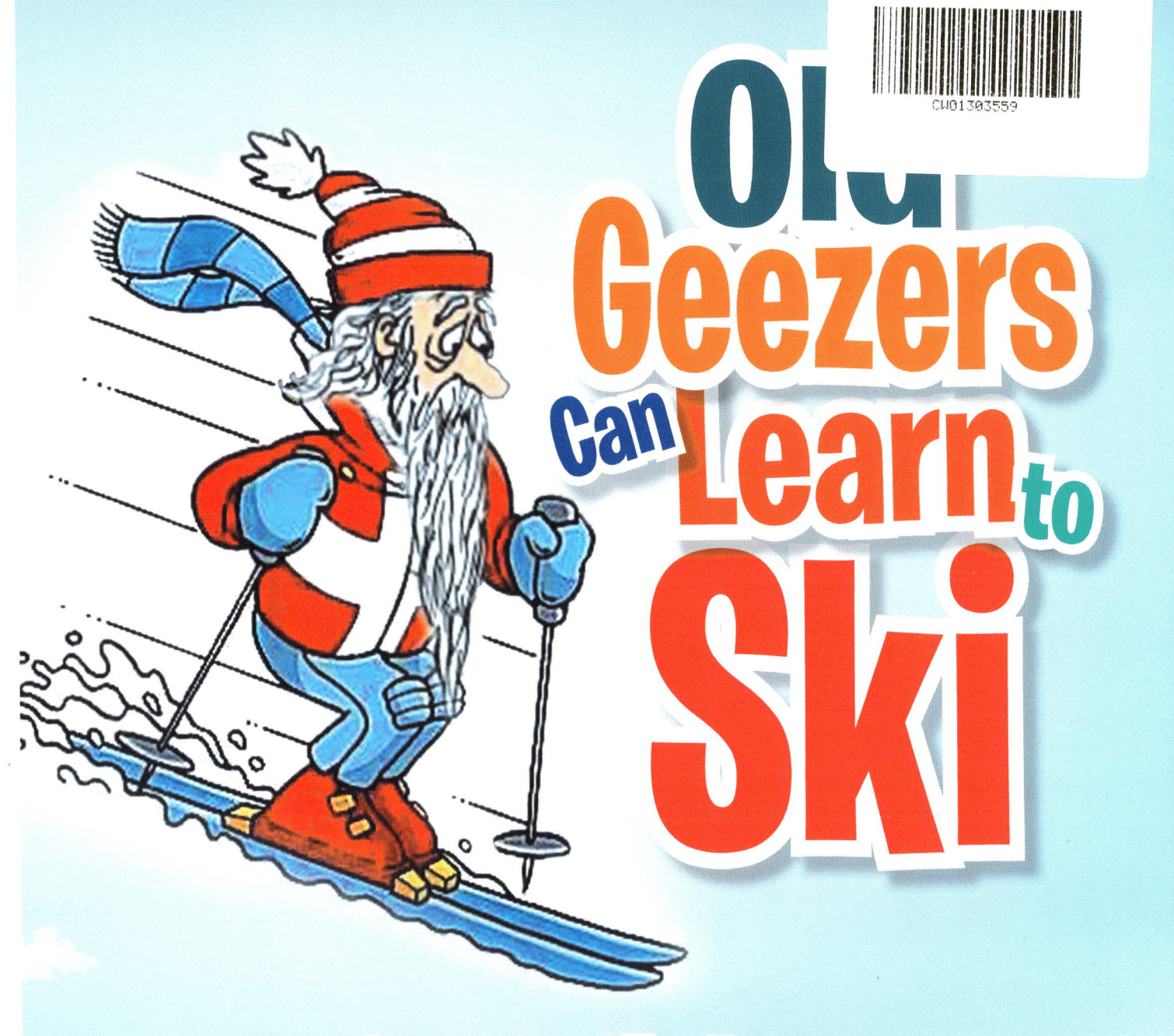

George Madsen

ILLUSTRATIONS BY DILLON BUCK

The GEEZER'S GUIDE to MODERN SKI TECHNIQUE

By George Madsen

For Seniors and Grandparents, the easy and safe way
to have fun on the ski slopes

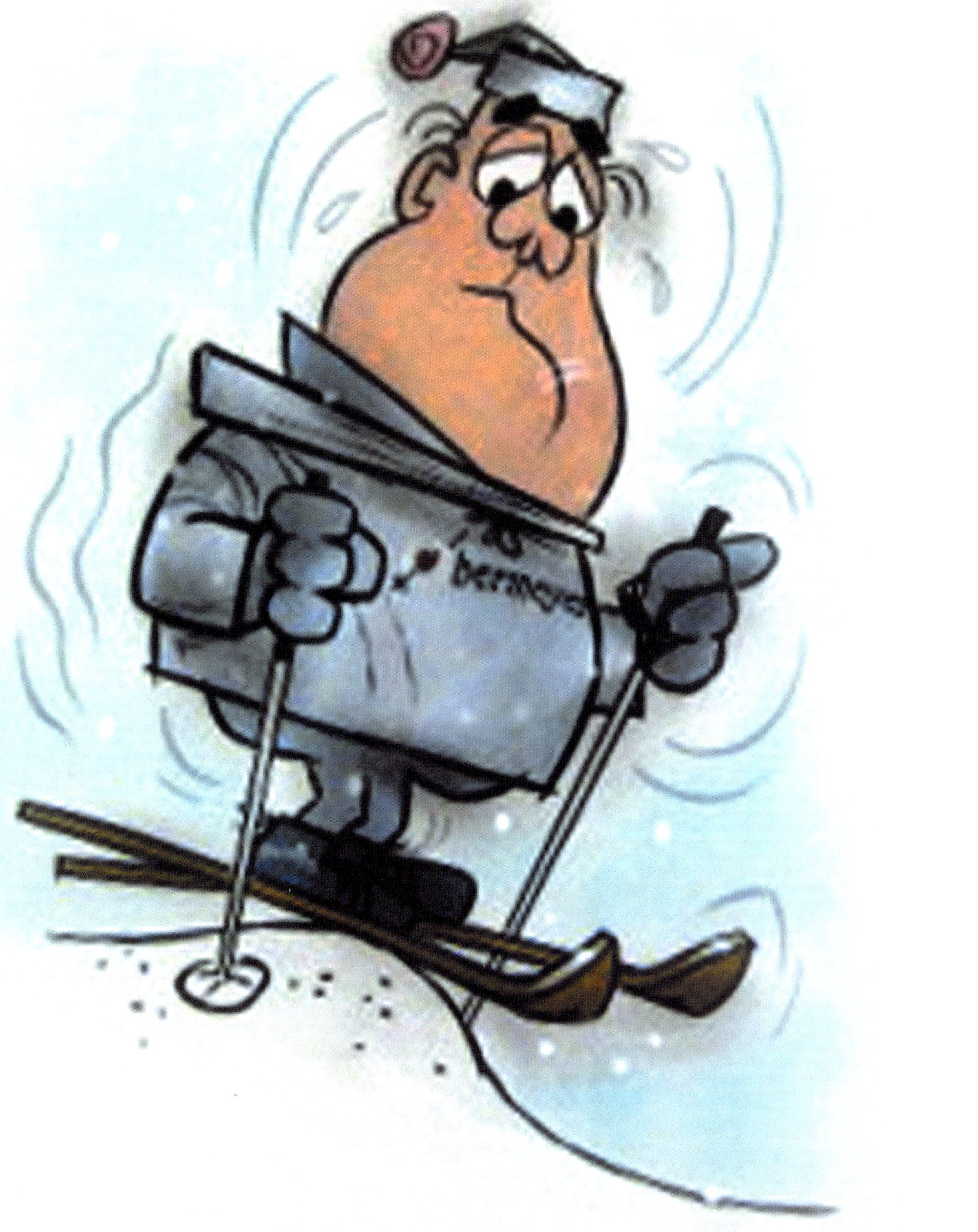

BACKWARD

I know. This part of a book is usually called the Foreword. But that's for a preface or introductory note. The Foreword is at the end of this volume because, hopefully, that's where we plan to go--on to new skiing experiences with confidence and anticipation of more fun.

If you're over 50, you've already got the credentials for a new or improved skiing career by age and experience alone. If you've never skied on snow, you may have water skied, jumped on a trampoline, played badminton, or wind surfed. OK, so you at least golfed, raked the lawn, stood on a ladder to wash your car, or put on your pants one leg at a time without falling over.

In a word, you've got some sense of BALANCE. That's what skiing is about--and about getting your nerve up to use balance to feel the exhilaration of sliding down a snowy hill in control.

But if you have skied before, you've got it made in the shade (to use a phrase, as I often do, that youths of today wouldn't understand). You learned about balance through the Arlberg Technique, Reverse Shoulder, Split Rotation, or the Toilet-paper Method (keeping your cheeks clamped together even without toilet paper never worked for me).

For the I-tried-it-once-and-want-to-try-it-again crew, the good news is that you've got the basics to advance to more modern and pleasurable, styles. Notice that I said styles, plural. There are as many ways to ski as there are human body configurations. Watch a professional golf match if you think the experts all swing to the same tune. You may wonder how they can teach one classic swing to neophytes.

The answer is they don't and they can't if they try to pour their students into their mold. But in skiing, if it feels comfortable, it'll probably work with only minor adjustments--without being moldy.

On the other hand, if you want to mimic a current Olympic champion, just drop 30 years off your age and pick up one of the hundreds of technical ski manuals that can explain how the champions do it.

Skiing can be as much fun for people who recognize the name of Alf Landon as for those who were taught to use computers in elementary school. It's just a matter of knowing your limitations--and opportunities.

I hope I can help.

CONTENTS

CHAPTER

I Ready, Set--Hold It! 7
   Are you in shape to ski? 7
II Getting Started. 11
   A. For the first time. 11
   B. For a better time 14
III Turning 21
   A. Easy stuff 22
   B. Moderate speed 23
   C. Fancy Dan. 25
IV More Turns 33
   A. Long. 34
   B. Short. 35
V Bumps 41
VI Powder 46
VII Ice, Heavy Wet Snow and Other Bad Stuff 50
VIII Equipment 54
   A. Boots 54
   B. Skis and bindings 56
   C. Poles. 58
   D. Clothing 58
IX Cross-country Skiing 64
X Miscellaneous and Everything Else . . . 68

TIPS

1 Pumping Up--strength and fluidity 10
2 Relax--then relax more 16
3 The big skier who said "I can!" 17
4 Cross-country sets the style 18
5 Beware of sun and wind 19
6 Rent before you buy 20
7 Get loose 27
8 How to fall and get up 28
9 PLEASE take a lesson. 29
10 Use your edge 30
11 Bend zee knees 31
12 Don't curl your toes 32
13 Watch the girls go by 37
14 Read the terrain 38
15 The new rotation 39
16 Relax 40
17 Moguls for everyone. 43
18 Know when to say no 44
19 Go back to basics 45
20 Ski in a storm 48
21 Be an old smoothie 49
22 Play it smart. 52
23 Go for the groomed 53
24 A good ski shop is a skier's best friend . . 60
25 Look good in the bar 61
26 Wonderful wool 62
27 Layer for comfort 63
28 Telemarking is worth the effort 66
29 Ski to a mountain hut 67

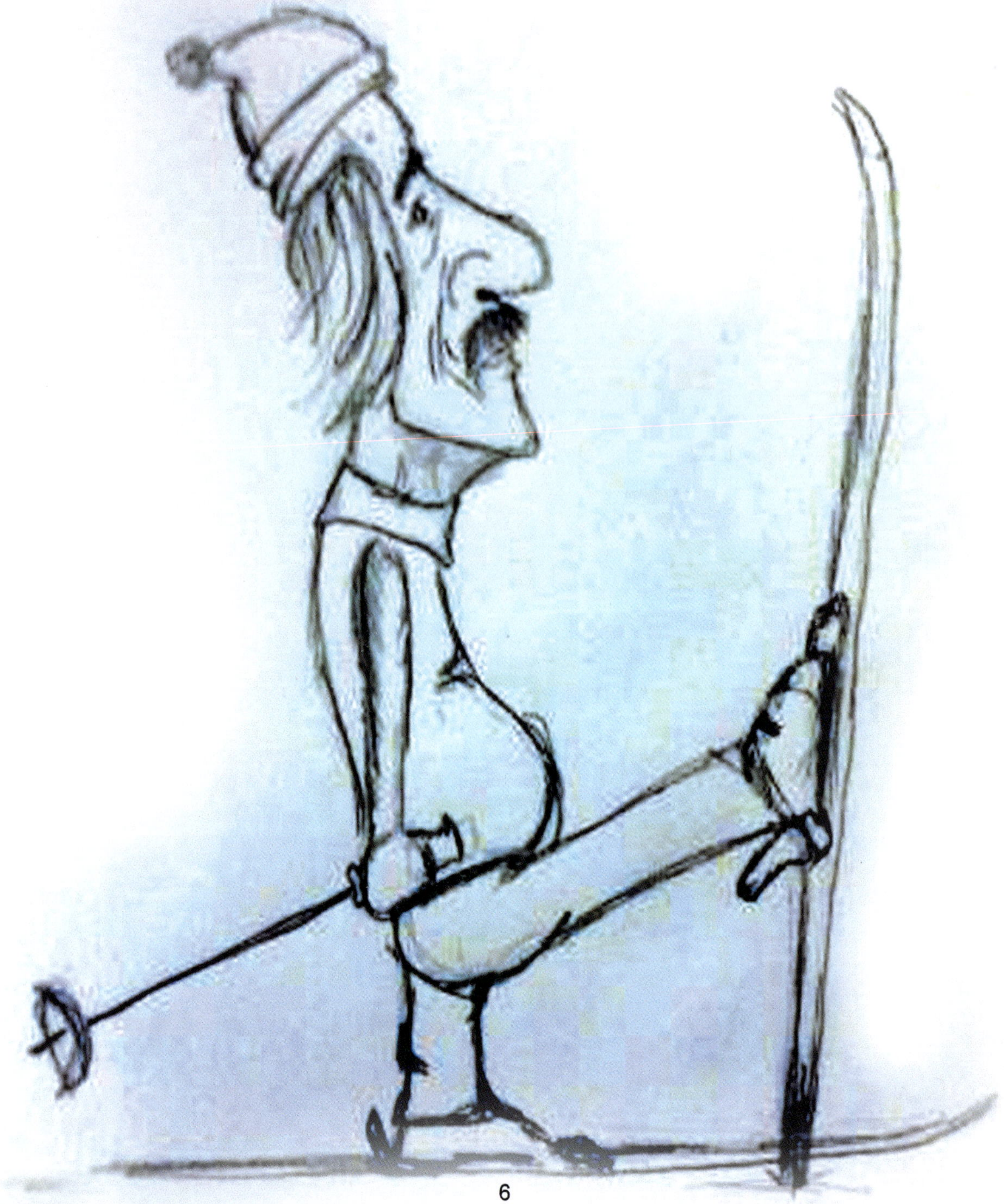

CHAPTER I

Ready, Set--Hold It!
Are you in shape to ski?

The good news is that if you can get into and out of your car without grunting excessively, you are probably strong enough to get up and down a beginner's ski slope. If you can do it several times in a minute, you're ready for intermediate terrain.

Golfers usually make good skiers, even if they use a cart, because both sports require concentration. But the better skiers can go 18 holes and they carry their bag or pull a cart. The energy they need is about the same as for a full day of skiing.

Most tennis players are physically comfortable on ski slopes, even if they only dabble in mixed doubles. Of course, those who are up for three sets are more comfortable than those who retire to the lounge after two.

If you have the patience to swat a badminton bird over a backyard net for a full game with a grade schooler, you have the coordination, agility and strength--with a little instruction--to tackle the slopes marked in green on a ski trail map.

Recreational skiers do not need to have bodies that are admired on Muscle Beach. But the sport definitely does take effort and enough physical fitness to produce that effort. Don't expect alpine skiing to trim the bulge in your waist during a week-long winter vacation. But it will keep you in shape if you are there already and you have the stamina to stay away from the ski-lodge bar.

This is not a plan for national Olympic-team candidates who train for 11 months a year. It isn't even a training plan for potential NASTAR recreational racers. It's a guide for seniors who want to get far enough up a mountain to watch ski racers in action, to view magnificent scenery from the top of mountains, and to enjoy the experience with other outdoor enthusiasts.

You're seeking enough knowledge of skiing to know what you are in for. But as philosopher John Locke noted, no man's knowledge can go beyond his experience.

So how do you prepare yourself physically for this experience? Answer: loosen up several times a week.

- Make it a point to walk when you can.
- Walk up stairs.
- Do a dozen knee bends, but don't bend your knees more than 90 degrees--that is, keep your heels touching the floor.
- Rotate your head, shoulders and arms a dozen times.
- Peck like a bird a dozen times.
- While standing, extend your arms to the sides and rotate them in little circles a dozen times, then the other way a dozen times.
- Same as above but make big circles.
- Do a dozen push-ups but with weight on your knees, not on your toes.
- On your back, grab your knees, and curl your feet back over your chest a dozen times.
- On one leg at a time, make one-quarter knee bends.
- Stand in a doorway and push against the sides of the passageway for 30 seconds.
- Swim and/or bike regularly.

These are just some of the ways to avoid the stiffness some wannabee skiers feel. Some of them may not be the answer for you. I may even be insulting the intelligence of some readers by suggesting these exercises. There are lots of good books, trainers and doctors who can formulate a program that will fit you better.

Maybe just regular sessions of racquetball or indoor tennis is all you need. The point is that skiing requires some physical assertiveness. You have to have more than the desire to ski to feel comfortable in getting into the sport.

Hey, don't push it. You may already be in shape. You're doing this to have fun, remember? So you may need an afternoon nap after your first morning on skis. So what, this is your vacation. You'll get stronger as your ski days progress. You may even feel good about needing a shower after skiing to remove the sweat instead of just improving your fragrance.

In short, the better shape you are in, the more you will enjoy the sport and the less chance you'll have of getting hurt.

One note of caution. Loosening up means GENTLY increasing your flexibility. Loosening up should not be interpreted as stretching till it hurts. Stretching may be OK when you are warm, after skiing or other exercise, but can be injurious when muscles are cold.

TIP NO. 1

Pumping Up--strength and fluidity

Let's put physical fitness into reasonable perspective. This is the Rambo era when bulging muscles and the body beautiful get admiration and Hans and Franz get laughs. Granted, today's athletes from high school to the professional ranks have better physical training than ever. But recreational skiers don't need to own a warehouse full of bar bells to enjoy the sport.

Some of the smoothest skiers I know are ladies in their 60s and 70s. They don't jump tall buildings or stop roaring freight trains. But they look like pros when they ski in the conditions they like and on the terrain they favor, even the tough stuff. They may not be agile and they sometimes grab the banister on a long flight of stairs. But they flow on ski runs.

Just about everyone can become a ski jock, and that definitely includes senior citizens. The body must be willing and the mind must be focused on what the body must perform. Enjoyable skiing is like good cooking--a combination of good ingredients and concentration. Oh yes, and a good cook book.

CHAPTER II

Getting Started

A. For the first time

Even if you've skied before, skim this. It sets the basics for the technique needed for not only beginners but also intermediate and advanced skiers.

Picture this. You are ice skating for the first time. You're on the edge of the rink holding onto anything or anyone. Now it's time for this bird to fly.

You take a tiny step and stop. Another step and stop. This is a delicate moon walk. Your feet appear to weigh 20 pounds apiece. No smile. You are bug-eyed with anticipation but becoming more brave. A step and a short glide. Two steps and coast. A little smile that reflects lingering fear. More stepping and coasting. You peer ahead because you don't dare look at your feet. And this time when you glide, you pigeon-toe your feet and grind to a stop. Soon you are putting your feet crossways to stop. Big grin, maybe even laughter.

Congratulations, you have just finished your first ski lesson. Your chest-high learner's skis are not as short as ice skates but they are fairly easy to handle. Several halting little steps. A short glide. Looking ahead, not at your feet. Wedging in a V to stop. Turning to stop. And some smiles.

Now let's translate that into ski technique. When going forward on level ground, you step just as in walking, and you swing your arms as you do when you walk. After a step, you glide. When you want to stop, you push out to a wedge--and keep pushing out to keep your tips from crossing as you gently slow down. Later, when your confidence and balance allow, you will turn your skis to skid to a stop.

That's probably how your instructor will get you moving. I assume you will have a professional instructor. Please don't let a friend or your Uncle Joe be your teacher. You paid plenty to be equipped and outfitted. A small percentage more for a professional instructor will protect your investment.

Previously, your instructor (he or she) checked the tightness of your boots, taught you how to get into and out of your bindings, and showed how to carry your skis (over your shoulder with tips forward). He told how to hold your poles (hand UP through the loop). He probably had you gliding, scooter style, on only one ski.

Two more exercises will make you an up-hiller before you advance to down-hilling. Side-step with little steps a short way up the bunny hill, keeping your skis parallel and directly across the slope. Next, using a reverse wedge, herringbone up slope with tiny steps. In both cases, you may have to edge your skis to prevent slipping (this is better explained by your instructor than described here).

Now you are ready to ski downhill and just far enough up the slope to try it. So assume the position that you will be in for the remainder of the lesson. It's the wedge position--a narrow wedge to move slowly and a wider one to slow down or stop. Stand tall and then bend your knees slightly. Your weight is on your whole foot (the ball of your foot and the heel) and if there is any question about how much weight is on the ball or heel, err towards the ball, not the heel. Stay forward. Never sit back.

You are now in balance on your skis. That's the function of the wedge and every skier uses it sometime during a ski day--even Olympian competitors (watch them wedge to slow down coming into lift lines). Try leaning forward and backward while in a wedge to see how much stability it offers. Now do the same thing with your feet parallel. Shaky, huh?

Now pretend you are a granite statue. Hands comfortably in front. Pole baskets behind you. And chin up with your eyes on the stretch pants of that cute person ahead of you. Got it? Now pose like a granite statue should. That's your first-day ski position--all day. Stay in the wedge and never-ever flail the air with your poles to avoid banishment back to square one.

Oh yes, you may want to turn to miss that skier in stretch pants or some other hazard. That's a simple maneuver because you've already mastered the fundamentals. Since you are in the wedge, one of your skis is pointing the way you want to go. Just twist it further in that direction and lighten up on the other ski. In some snow conditions, you may want to put some pressure on your twisting ski by leaning ever so lightly on it. But don't lean much. Instead, muscle that ski around with your foot.

To some new skiers, turning skis may seem unnatural. That's understandable. In ice skating and riding a bicycle, you lean inside on a turn. In skiing you lean slightly outside. In addition, when skaters point their skates in a different direction, they expect to go in that direction immediately. When bikers turn their handlebars, they know they will go off in a new direction at once. It's different in skiing--particularly in novice skiing. Turning takes longer. A twisting ski has to turn far enough to use the full force of its length before the turn is accomplished. That's why lightening the weight on the inside ski is so important--so it won't hinder the turning action of the pressured turning ski.

That may sound complicated. I apologize. I vowed I would keep this essay non-technical. But I hope you get the idea. Maybe I can straighten you out in the next chapter.

GETTING STARTED

B. For a better time

This chapter is for people who have skied before--even those who disliked their previous forays on the slopes--and attempts to show what is new, exciting and safer in the modern technique and ski experience. Perhaps you were forced into returning to the sport because you are sick of festering in a condo while your kids and grandkids have all the fun you are paying for. Or maybe you've had a mid-life crisis and now are ready to roll and show those young rockers a thing or two.

Regardless of your reasons, you've made a good decision because skiing today is probably different, easier and more fun than you remember. It's also more expensive. So listen up and read what you can expect to get for your money.

In a nutshell, modern technique is based on the availability of superior equipment designed by rocket scientists and snow grooming that is the envy of golf-course greens keepers. That ought to ease some of your apprehensions.

Here is what you will be taught in ski school during your course of instruction from where you left off to where you gain the comfort and degree of confidence you require.

- Stand tall--don't hunch over

- Bend zee knees but not too much, especially in turns

- Turning movements are mainly made by your lower body--legs, knees and feet

- Use less up-down movement in turns and more to and fro (forward and slightly back)

- Pole plant or pole touch opposite your toe, not by the shovel of your ski

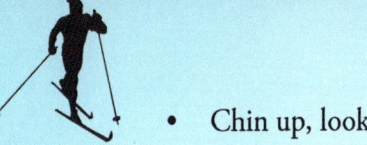

- Chin up, look ahead
- Relax your whole body

That's it, or mostly it. Everything else remains the same. You may even find that the basics haven't changed--they just have new and fancy names. But if the new terminology makes you yawn, ask your instructor to explain "anticipation" and what "dynamic" means. The answer may take a few more ski vacations to figure out.

Let me try to give you an historical perspective of how much has changed since you last skied. If that was ten years ago, the movements and positions are pretty much the same but a number of refinements, or ways of explaining basic movements, have been added.

Twenty years ago, the vestiges of shoulder rotation, which is mainly deemphasized now, were still evident. More important, the techniques taught by ski schools were as diverse as their geographical locations. It could be difficult to continue the format of instruction you got on the East Coast with that offered in the Midwest, Rockies, West Coast, and Canada--or any combination of those regions.

Thirty years ago, the same as above and add to that the dramatic reverse-shoulder style which was popularized by Olympic racers.

Forty years ago--do you really want to discuss ancient history that will emphasize your ancientness?--the Arlberg Technique was the norm as it was in the 1930s and 40s. If you still ski this way, you definitely need a lesson for your personal protection. Steel edges and safety bindings were in their infancy and grooming was something you did in the bathroom to look pretty.

If all this sends you into a fit of senility, think how a 1960s Olympic medalist felt when he recently viewed a film documenting his past achievement. "I didn't know I skied that badly," he moaned.

But, of course, he didn't have the advantage of modern equipment, grooming and technique. You have. And since you have the desire to return to this crazy sport, do it. You may eventually ski better than an Olympic champion once did.

TIP NO. 2

Relax--then relax more

Relax! How can I say it differently for more emphasis? Loosen up. Unglue. Give it some slack. Lighten up. Cool it. Take it easy. Time out. Unzip. Don't strain. Take a breath. Simmer down.

Good skiers are relaxed. Poor skiers are up tight. I won't say you can't learn to ski well if you are stiff and wooden, but it would be a miracle if you did. It's natural for skiers to be apprehensive on the bunny slope or a black-diamond trail. But they will flounder if they are excessively fearful.

There are a number of ploys good instructors use to try to dissipate anxiety. But the final solution to the problem rests with the skier himself. No skier is fearless in every situation. However, the sport isn't any fun for people who are needlessly scared.

Try this. Each time you stop, exhale, lower your shoulders, and consciously let tension drain out of your muscles. Capture that feeling and let it happen often.

Sure, this exercise requires concentration. But concentration is an essential element of skiing. One of the most fearless "extreme skiers" I know concentrates on exhaling through every turn because, he says, he can't "feel" his skis when he is tense. And he needs to feel his skis to avoid extreme catastrophe.

TIP NO. 3

The big skier who said "I can!"

You remember the children's story about the little engine that said "I think I can, I think I can!" It was successful because of a positive mental attitude.

In contrast, I remember a student named Gloria, resplendent in a white one-piece ski suit and enough jewelry to open a boutique, who confided to me before her first ski lesson, "I'm not going to like this." She didn't and was last seen striding toward the base lodge with her skis under her arm. That was after one run down the bunny slope.

Skiers who do make it down the bunny hill are sometimes frustrated because they can turn only to the left and not to the right. Or they can't glide to a stop fast enough. Frustration isn't terminal for skiers. In fact, it's probably an inherent problem in learning anything.

I think you get my message--proper mental attitude is essential for making skiing fun. Ski instructors appreciate gung-ho students and usually give more attention to pupils who make an effort to carry on after they have fallen. And once they get it, these students often progress more rapidly than others.

TIP NO. 4

Cross-country sets the style

Novice downhill skiers, or experienced alpine skiers who need a refresher, can learn a good lesson about balance by trying cross-country skiing. And, as I've preached previously, balance is the key to all skiing.

Walking on cross-country skis, if you take short steps, is just like the beginner exercise on alpine skis, only you can lift your heel. Your arms and poles move the same way--that is, your right arm and right leg move ahead at the same time and, of course, ditto on the left side. You stride as in walking.

Also, when you want to slow down or stop, you wedge in a V, just as you do on downhill skis. However, cross-country skis are much lighter and cross-country boots are as light as tennis sneakers or light-duty hiking boots. As a result, when you fall down, it's much easier to get up--either by removing the ski as in downhill skiing or by using a few gymnastic movements.

Even some elements of skating and telemarking on Nordic skis are closely related to alpine skiing. But that's another story. You'll enjoy the exhilaration of cross-country skiing without trying to scale mountains and ski down them.

TIP NO. 5

Beware of sun and wind

What works for me is sunglasses and adequate amounts of sun tan cream and lip balm all winter long, even when the sun is low in December and January. In stormy weather, I switch from sunglasses to goggles but still apply sun cream and lip balm.

I find that sun cream and lip balm provide moisture which prevents wind burn. If you happen to be male, you have another option--grow a mustache that collects snow which melts from body temperature to keep you kissable. Skiers with a light complexion might consider wearing a ski mask.

In spring when I sometimes wear a baseball cap, I put sun tan cream on my ears. And when I eat outside in warm weather, I put cream on the back of my hands.

One other idea which may not appeal to you--I wear a ski hat with a short brim to keep the sun off the usually unprotected area on my lower forehead. Looks funny but is effective. Of course, I put tanning cream there as well, which you should do unless you have a penchant for Arabian head gear.

TIP NO. 6
Rent before you buy

Ski shops and specialty stores that rent equipment have come a long way forward in the last 15 years. Not only is the equipment better, especially for new skiers and those re-entering the sport, but shop personnel generally have the technical training and positive attitude to correctly match up skiers and their specific needs.

Shop workers--they prefer to be called ski mechanics--know how to fit boots, select skis that fit a skiers ability or lack of it, and choose poles that are the correct length. Furthermore, they usually are a good source of information about skiing and their local area.

For more advanced skiers, stores that rent often have a good selection of demos, but these models are best at the beginning of the season when they are still factory-tuned. It's always best to try out skis before you purchase them.

However, renters, like buyers, should beware. When you are being fitted into boots, make sure you understand the purpose of all the gadgets that adjust fit. For skis, learn how to get into and out of bindings. As you become more proficient in skiing, get longer boards but don't move up more than 10 centimeters at a time. For both boots and skis, memorize the shop identification numbers on your equipment so you don't get them mixed up with someone else's that look the same.

Rental shops are extremely busy over the Christmas holidays and in high season. They also may be sold out of popular sizes. So button up your rental requirements before you need to use the gear.

CHAPTER III

Turning

Skiing is a turning sport--for everyone from beginner to expert. Turning is the fun part. If you can't turn, you can't have fun. You certainly can't go up the mountain because you are relegated to the bunny slopes. Of course, it's also the necessary part that allows you to avoid calamity, to be free to go where you want, and, most important, to permit you to stop.

Have you ever heard of anyone who was happy plunging straight down a hill and continued to return for more year after year? Never.

In modern ski technique, developing ability is a matter of learning more advanced turning skills, and each progression is based on what you learned in the previous progression.

This chapter is written with the assumption that you intend to take a ski lesson each time you want to turn better and have more fun. It's impossible for a text like this to relate precisely to the instructional needs of people of every physical shape and mental acuity, so I won't try. Instead, my purpose is to present the simple basics so that you will know what to expect at each stage of progress. Your instructor can address your special, personal needs.

TURNING

A. Easy stuff

In the previous chapter, I explained that positioning your skis in a wedge or V shape is the basic maneuver to keep your balance in running, turning and stopping. A narrow wedge lets you run faster, a wider wedge slows you down and permits you to stop, and any kind of a wedge gives you the ability to turn if you twist your right foot to turn left, put more weight on your right foot, and take some weight off the left foot. Of course, for a right turn you do just the opposite.

As you do this, your forearms are parallel to the slope and you are holding your poles lightly so that the baskets on the poles are behind you--not straight up and down as so many beginners do with evidently the mistaken idea that if they start to fall, they can jab their poles into the snow to regain balance. That action destroys proper balance. The poles get in your way and can cause a tumble.

Your chin is up and you are looking ahead to your next turn. You are a skiing statue, leaning only slightly forward and to the outside of the turn, and primarily using your feet to turn in the direction you want to go. The shape of the wedge--narrow or wide--is keeping you in balance and controlling your speed.

Initiate your turn slowly. Don't jack yourself around. Twist your turning foot and wait for the skis to start in the new direction. In soft or wet snow, your skis will turn quickly. When the snow is hard, it will take a little longer for the skis to bite to make a turn and you'll have to make a strong wedge to stop.

In addition to turning, you have just found a new way to stop. When your skis are pointed across the slope, you slow down because you are no longer going down the hill. Simple, right? Now try this to the other side. This is the main method of stopping you will use for the rest of your ski days and a major key to advanced skiing.

B. Moderate speed

Now that you have mastered the basic wedge turn, you are ready for a little more speed and some movements to control increased speed. But you still need all the elements that you employed in learning the wedge. You're on your way toward skiing more parallel and the wedge will get you there.

Since you have to ski faster, you need a slightly steeper hill. But make sure there's a run-out at the bottom so you can slow down if you get in trouble. Try your wedge turn here. Notice that you must put more muscle in your turns to get your skis around. Also note that your skis skid sideways a little more as you turn. Relax, this is the way it's supposed to be. You can still ski across the slope to slow down.

But you will find that it is more difficult to stay in the wedge when you ski across the hill--that is, when you ski at a right angle to straight down the hill. The technical term for this is "crossing the fall line." The fall line is straight down--where a basketball would go if you dropped it when you skied across the slope. And wedging across the fall line is difficult because the hill is steeper and your uphill ski is higher than your downhill ski.

So it's only natural that now you must make a very narrow wedge or even put your skis together in a parallel position. Do it. Then get into the wedge as you turn the other way. That's how skiing is done--turning one way and then the other. It's the way you check your speed, by making small (short radius) turns and traversing (going across the hill) to slow down.

In the basic wedge, your feet are directly under your elbows. Now you are in a narrower wedge and your feet are closer together--under your shoulders when you traverse. You may be comfortable with your feet even closer together as you progress but you should never lock your feet together. Although separation may make the heart grow fonder, feet need independence much more than togetherness. A large part of moving up the skiing proficiency ladder is understanding how feet interact with each other in turning.

Remember that your body position remains relatively constant--chin up, hands in front, pole baskets behind. And now you can stand a little taller because your wedge is narrower and your feet closer together.

If you can do that smoothly and comfortably, in a few days try bringing your skis together earlier in the turn and developing a little skid sideways as you start to traverse. Increase the skid without leaning uphill. Now you are wedging as you begin a turn, holding the wedge a moment until you get just past the fall line, moving your feet closer together and skidding sideways as you start into the traverse, and holding that position with your feet even a tad closer until you start a new turn the other way.

Take a bow. Your skiing ability has shown great improvement and you may not have realized it. You have developed a Power Foot and Power Leg (and Power Ski)--that's your outside or downhill foot and leg--because you needed to give them more oompf to get around in the turn. And you lightened and almost lifted the uphill foot to move it nearly parallel with your Power Foot because that was the easiest way to get that ski out of the way of your Power Ski.

You're catching on fast but there are still a couple of movements needed to complete this phase of your skiing. Notice that you are automatically swinging your arms a little. That's good--the statue has come to life and your whole body is getting into the act and developing rhythm. When you are in the middle of a turn, your outside or downhill arm has moved slightly forward and will stay that way until you start to traverse. Now, with wrist action, bring the tip of the pole in that hand forward, touch it lightly in the snow outside and a little ahead of your downhill ski boot, ski past it and let it come out of the snow naturally as you ski past.

You have just completed your first pole plant. But never let either hand fall out of sight when you are turning and planting a pole. Keep your hands in front--and in the corner of your eye--for balance. If your hands go back too far, you go back on your skis and you can't turn sitting back. Getting slightly forward on your skis while you are skiing on your whole foot also comes automatically because you need to be forward to give your Power Foot and Leg the emphasis they require to drive you through a turn.

Something else is happening automatically. You are probably bending your knees more when you complete a turn simply to absorb the force of the change of direction. Wonderful. Now stand tall again so that your skis will be easier to turn in your next change of direction. The faster you ski, the more you turn, sink and stand tall. This used to be a called an up-down motion when it was practiced more aggressively on ungroomed slopes. The old term still fits but the movement lacks the gusto of yesteryear.

There is one thing that is not automatic but should be practiced when conditions warrant. When you are making a series of little turns down the fall line on groomed snow, keep both shoulders downhill and in the fall line as much as is comfortably possible. This happens naturally in big, swooping turns, except in traverses, of course. But in little turns it needs to be remembered because the turning action is quicker and there isn't time to keep turning your shoulders to wave to your friends.

C. Fancy Dan

The following suggestions are intended to help you become the best skier you can be--considering your senior citizen status. That's a very important caveat. Your physical condition, combined with your degree of aggressiveness (or lack of aggressiveness) may make you more comfortable in wedging a little in your turns. You can't be called chicken for following that route. Quite the contrary, you're playing it smart. Even top skiers wedge sometimes.

I have a confession to make. Over 30 years ago when I took a foreign job assignment in mid-state Illinois, I played a lot of golf and I learned to play quite well because that was the game of choice in the flatlands. Since moving to the mountains, I play recreational golf occasionally, mainly to keep company with my grown kids during the summer. I stink. I'm lucky if I'm only 20 shots worse for 18 holes than I was in my prime. In fact, the only time I score well is when I skip the Fancy Dan stuff and go back to the simple basics I learned as a caddy in my youth. That's the only time I have fun, too.

Got the message? Do what you feel comfortable doing. Don't push yourself too far. That works for me in tennis because my reactions are still pretty good, just as they are in skiing. But I don't try to smash the big first serve every time. Instead, I cut my serve into the corners and don't rush to the net to volley as I once did. And in skiing, I don't always crash down the fall line in a mogul field but prefer to ride out the first bump and turn on another that's more to my liking.

In short, your score in golf identifies your ability. In skiing, nobody is keeping score and, as in tennis, you do your best when you do what's comfortable. We're still into skiing for fun, aren't we?

With that disclaimer, here are three simple ways to hone your skiing technique and make you a fancier Dan. First, do exactly what you have been doing but do it better. Second, exert your Power Leg more aggressively and ski almost as if you are skating by powering one leg at a time. And third, use more forward motion with your upper body when you launch--almost dive--into a turn.

Perhaps this sounds simple but it may not be. It depends on the first point--how much you've really progressed so far. I'll explain that comment shortly but first I want to tell a story.

An Irish lass--I'd guess she was in her early 40s--was my private lesson student for two hours recently. She was a fine, parallel skier, had skied all over Europe, but wasn't comfortable with her current skiing even though her friends marveled at her form. She reminded me of myself when I was shooting good golf but not as good as I thought I could.

I told her I thought she was leaning slightly into the hill--that is, leaning uphill--probably because she was a bit rusty in this early season, and we skied through several exercises together to try to correct the problem. No solution yet. Then I told her to follow me making lazy turns and dragging her outside or downhill pole. Drag it hard and make a mark in the snow, I insisted. Eureka! She finally got her weight far enough over her Power Ski so that she felt in control. We both smiled but she smiled more.

The point of the story is that she got back to the niche in which she was comfortable. I use this to validate the first point--do what you are already doing better. You got a Bachelor's Degree in the wedge. Now earn a Master's Degree in the same turn but with a narrower wedge. Do it on steeper slopes and in loose snow. Make believe you are in a slalom course and do it more rapidly in a series of turns. When the terrain is steeper and your speed is faster, it's easier to get parallel quicker. It's only natural--and more comfortable.

Second, make a medium-sized turn the way you normally do but as soon as you start to move across the fall line--that is, as soon as you are no longer skiing straight down the hill-- put most of you weight, without leaning your body, on your downhill ski and pick up the heel of your lightened uphill ski. Throughout this maneuver, pay close attention to keeping your uphill ski parallel with your Power Ski.

Remember, this is an exercise to keep you in balance when you are going faster. Now, since your skis are more parallel much earlier in the turn, you will ski faster in the turn. You definitely should accelerate in the turn and traverse to slow down. But you have heard that before. If you didn't get it then, your increased speed makes it easier to comprehend now.

And third, once you start turning, move your upper body a little more forward and into the turn to assist your acceleration and make your turn smoother. This is not really diving into the turn. It's a small but important weight adjustment for only this part of the turn. If you do it correctly, it will feel as if your body is pulling you into the turn.

Of course, how quickly you become a Dapper Dan skier depends on how well you have mastered the rudiments. But since you've come this far, you're a good bet to make it soon.

TIP NO. 7

Get loose

Skiing has an advantage over many other sports--it usually has built-in loosening up movements. That's when you are forced to lug your heavy gear from the parking lot to the lifts. You dread it, but it's an easy and effective way to get your juices flowing. You don't want to start skiing when you're stiff and cold.

I've suggested a few pre-season exercises in Chapter I that will also serve in the mornings before you head for the slopes. Now you are on your way to the base lift. Put your boots on loosely, but tight enough so that you can't lift your heel very much. If the distance isn't too great, walking in your boots with your skis on your shoulder and your poles in hand warms you up for your ski day.

Of course, you'll want to tighten your boots when you are ready to ski. With your skis on but before your first run, wave your arms in a big circle one way and then the other. Standing tall, lean back a little and feel muscles that you may not know you have. Hold the position for a few seconds. Do the same thing by leaning forward. Do several shallow (not deep) knee bends with each leg.

Start down the slope fairly slowly and make a series of easy turns that re-introduce you to other muscles. No problem, right? And you owe it all to that forced march from the parking lot that you now grudgingly appreciate.

TIP NO. 8

How to fall and get up

"How to fall" usually takes care of itself. You do it--period. But students often ask, when they feel themselves going over and have an option of which way they crash, what should they do. The answer is to fight falling as long as you can but, if you must go down, give up completely, be relaxed, and fall backwards. The worst thing you can do is to fall sideways and roll. Definitely avoid rolling over and digging your knees into the snow.

The above works pretty well at slow speeds. The higher your speed, the less options you have. But when you feel a fall about to happen at any speed, relax! And don't stab you poles into the snow in an effort to stay upright. That's a good way to get hurt.

Getting up after falling on any slope that has a medium or steep pitch is easy. Put your feet below you, make your skis parallel and across the slope (at a right angle to the fall line), and shove yourself up with your arms or poles. If your skis came off in the fall, put your downhill ski on first for better balance.

Getting up on easy or flat terrain is more difficult because your feet are on about the same level with your body and rising takes considerably more effort. Still, follow the procedure suggested above and if your body is unwilling to move, release your bindings, stand up, and put on your skis. The fun part comes at the end of the day when you describe your entanglements and grossly exaggerate your difficulties.

Note: My physical fitness experts inform me that falling while totally relaxed can cause ligament injuries, and that falling when tense may cause muscle injuries which are less serious. That may well be true. But what I've witnessed in 50-some years of skiing is that skiers who keep their speed under control, relax and fall backwards when they lose balance--and don't roll--hardly ever sustain injuries that can't be fixed with a warm kiss on the cheek.

TIP NO. 9

PLEASE take a lesson

You probably think that I'm just trying to hard-sell my own professional bag of goods. Maybe so. But I'm also making a plea to learn skiing's basic movements so that you can have lots of fun with perhaps fewer lessons. Believe me, it's no fun for instructors who are asked to dig intermediates out of ruts that they should have learned as beginners. You don't need to take your instructor out to lunch. Just show him/her that you have the fundamentals which he can use to help you improve.

So I'll tell you two sad stories and let you draw your own conclusions. First, I tried to teach an athletic 30-year-old man who rated himself at Level 7 on a scale of 1 to 9. He had no trouble keeping up as he jammed both skis into every short turn with the grace of a tractor driver. And he announced that he wanted to increase his speed on the toughest Black Diamond slopes.

His problem was that skiing fast and making quick, jerky turns was all he could do. He actually could not swing through a big, lazy turn and he refused to go slower. My problem was that I didn't want to assist in his suicide. I suggested that he get his money back or find another instructor.

The other story concerns a girl in her mid-20s, a novice who had skied five times over a two-year period, all under the tutelage of her boyfriend. This was her second try this year. She said she joined a beginner's class because she wasn't progressing. The rest of the class graduated from the beginner's hill after two days. It took her three days--she needed two days just to overcome bad habits.

TIP NO. 10
Use your edge

In this case, your edge is on your ski and it's made of steel. When your skis are tilted or canted in a turn or traverse (a movement called "edging"), steel edges make them hold their line much better than skis that are flat on the snow. And when you want to stop quickly, you'll bless the steel beneath you.

Edging is a delicate maneuver and is usually easier for young, athletic people than for seniors who have less mobility. For beginners and intermediates, it is employed in small doses. But it definitely needs to be used. Furthermore, it's a natural movement. If you are hiking across a steep slope, you edge your hiking boots into the bank to keep from slipping down the hill. But you don't lean into the hill or the edge of your boots will give way and your feet will slide out from under you.

It's the same with skis. The way to "set an edge" is to press your knees uphill but keep your body over your skis in a balanced position. Remember that on steep slopes your skis are naturally edged by the steepness of the slope even if your feet are squarely under you. That's why edging is a delicate maneuver. You have to practice it to get the feel of how much is enough for each movement.

Beginners who are wedging to stop with their skis flat on hard snow should get in a knock-kneed position in order to use their edges to stop faster. Intermediates will naturally edge their outside or downhill ski in turns at normal speeds on intermediate runs. And advanced skiers usually turn by edging both skis, a maneuver that can be assisted by some reverse or counter hip movement (opposite to the direction of the turn) and is sometimes difficult for seniors who have less mobility than younger skiers.

TIP NO. 11

Bend zee knees

The full expression popularly attributed to Austrian ski instructors in the 1930s, 40s and 50s was "Bend zee knees and follow me." I'm old enough to remember that admonition if that's what they actually said. But my memory has slipped a gear and I don't recall hearing the phrase. However, if they did, those ski meisters were as modern as tomorrow and students should follow their advice today.

But there's a difference in modern times. Still follow your instructor but bend zee knees less since you don't have to put as much power into your turns as you did when slopes were ungroomed and skis were as inflexible as railroad ties. Flexing your knees too much has a tendency to cause excessive bending at the waist and an effort to force the skis through a turn with the upper body rather than with the legs and feet.

Today, the emphasis is on standing tall with a little knee flex, with extension of the downhill leg in turns to put pressure on that ski, and with moving your body slightly forward in a turn and back to center as you complete it. The new technique, tailored to the today's conditions and equipment, requires a lot less muscle. But don't tell your grandkids. Impress them with stories about how you had to struggle in the good old days.

TIP NO. 12

Don't curl your toes

Picture yourself. You are a fashion plate in the beginner's class with your bright purple rented boots and a one-piece outfit that makes you feel like a sky diver. And then your instructor says, "OK, Fred, your next. Let's see you make a wedge turn." You immediately tense up--and your toes curl up. Even after you graduate from the beginner's hill, your toes still curl when you peer down an intermediate slope.

I don't know why it happens but it often does. Maybe it's just one of those peculiar idiosyncrasies that goes with skiing. But it doesn't help your skiing because you can't curl your toes without tensing the muscles in your lower leg. To ski better, you must be relaxed, not tense anyplace.

The only solution is to be aware of your toe curl and set your mind to uncurl. Stand on your relaxed full foot. Feel the ball of your foot and the heel. Just as you can talk yourself into doing something that may seem stupid at the time, talk yourself out of curling your toes. It's your problem to correct. Your instructor can't see what's going on in your bright purple rented boots.

CHAPTER IV

More Turns

At this stage in your skiing experience, you are skiing parallel or nearly parallel--probably pretty parallel on easy slopes and wedging on steeper ones. Don't worry about how parallel you are now. You may keep your skis together on a left turn and wedge slightly going to the right, or vice versa. Don't let this really minor problem trouble you--you are not taking an exam to become an instructor. You are still trying to move closer to your potential as a senior skier and you may be more comfortable with waltzing than hard rocking.

We're still talking basics here and no one is keeping score. If what I am suggesting below doesn't feel comfortable for your personal physical limitations and abilities, you may need fine tuning by an instructor. But if you employ only a smidgen of some of these movements--or at the least, understand what the movement is meant to achieve--you can't help but improve.

Keep in mind that many aspects of long and short turns are the same. However, they are different mainly because you have less time to execute short turns and, as a result, some of the nice, fun stuff of long turns must be eliminated when you make short-radius turns.

A few years ago, one of the students in my class was a 60-something gentleman who paid for his retirement by building shopping malls in Florida. He had a command-type executive personality which drove me and the rest of the class batty. He was forever demanding why-this and why-not-that. But we got along fairly well, mainly because I gave him some back-talk which was the only thing he seemed to respect. At the end of the day, he confided to me, "I think I've got it--this is a thinking man's sport." Indeed it is. With a wry smile, I suggested he would have learned more if he had realized this at the beginning of the lesson--as any high-powered executive should.

MORE TURNS

A. Long

A long turn places you ten yards or more down the slope from where you started turning. It's sometimes called a GS or giant slalom turn and it's probably the same radius turn you been making previously. But now you are on steeper terrain--the intermediate trails marked with blue squares or the black-diamond trails for experts--and you need more finesse to handle them smoothly.

Smoothness is what you are striving for in long turns. And because they are long, you have some time to think your turns through. The first thing you think about is making your turn round. You do not abruptly change direction. As I've pointed out before, you initiate the turn, keep the pressure on, and then ride out the turn until you are going across the hill and preparing for your next turn. Furthermore, you accelerate in the turn and slow down when traversing. Achieving smoothness is as much regulating your speed as making fully controlled movements.

The important controlled movements you make in a long turn are the same as you have always made but slightly exaggerated because you are moving faster and need to supply more punch. That is, you stand tall and a little forward and squarely on your feet to feel both the ball and heel of your foot throughout the turn; you extend, but don't stiffen, your downhill leg to put more pressure on that ski which will carve the turn; you edge that downhill ski as needed to keep your skis from slipping sideways; and you sink (bend your knees) slightly to soak up the pressure in your legs that the turn has generated.

But there are other movements that provide finesse to make your turn smoother. Although most of the pressure is on your downhill ski, you should consciously steer your uphill ski to keep it parallel with your downhill ski. As you ski straight down the fall line and turn across the fall line, your skis should be slightly more turned than your shoulders (in other words, your shoulders are slightly delayed, a minor version of the reverse shoulder technique that was once popular). And as you cross the fall line and move into a traverse, your chest should move back a couple of inches and then move forward again as you move into the next turn the other way.

You'll notice that I frequently use terms like "slightly," "a little," and "a couple of inches." I mean exactly that. These movements should not be exaggerated. Learning them is a matter of "feel" and are best practiced on what you consider is a relatively easy slope for your talents. You don't need a great deal of speed to get the proper feel. "Feel" is proper when you are comfortable in performing the movement. Try it slowly at first and go faster at your own discretion.

One other thing that people who have too much already to remember often forget--in preparation for a turn, touch your downhill pole in the snow opposite and a little ahead of your downhill boot and then ski past it for a couple of yards before you start turning your feet. The function of a pole touch is to automatically position your body for turn initiation. If you are skiing fast, you don't need to touch the pole to the snow but you should still make a swing with your arm as if you were going to touch it.

B. Short

Time is of the essence is this turn. You don't have as much of it as you do in long turns. Therefore, you skip or restrict some long-turn frills. Whereas long turns are best suited to giant slalom racing, short turns are used in slalom competition where the slalom poles are much closer together. But I'm still not trying to make you into a go-for-broke racer. Short turns for recreational skiers are used wherever you want but particularly on steeper terrain and in narrow corridors of trails.

So what do you do? You link your turns with a very short traverse. As much as possible, you keep your shoulders facing downhill and in the fall line. You use your legs more, especially in up-down movements (bending your knees to complete a turn and rising to start the next turn), and use your body less--that is, keep your body forward as usual but relatively stationary. You press down on the tip of your downhill (outside) ski when you turn, a movement that makes you stay forward. Turns are made mainly with your downhill ski and the uphill (inside) ski is lightened considerably. You may even lift the tail of your uphill ski (to make your uphill ski parallel with your downhill ski) and let your downhill ski do all the work.

In spite of all these aberrations, you still employ all the basic positions--stand tall, hands in sight and lower arms at a right angle to your body, feel both the ball and heel of your feet, and stay in balance. There's no time for a to-and-fro movement of your body. In fact, you can bid adios to your balance if you lean back at all. You just don't have time to recover your balance.

You are paying good money for your ski poles whether they are bought or rented and short turns afford the opportunity to cash in on your investment. Use them decisively. This is the time to plant your poles instead of just touching them to the snow. Planting a pole is not a jab. It's like putting a fork into a piece of meat that you are carving. You don't want the meat to get away nor do you want to splash juice onto the table cloth. So you insert your pole into the snow up to the basket, and start turning immediately. And at almost the same time, ready the other pole for your next turn in the other direction by lifting the tip and pointing it at the next target.

All this may sound more difficult than it really is. As in all recreational skiing maneuvers, you're trying to establish rhythm. If you make it easy on yourself and try to get into the rhythm of short turns on a smooth slope of moderate pitch, it isn't too hard to get the knack of it.

However, there is one very important movement that gives some skiers trouble. In short turns you must look, not at the turn you are making, but at the place where you want to make the next turn. You put your feet on automatic pilot and have confidence that they will remember what they are supposed to do while you look ahead for their next starring role. You do this in hiking so why not in skiing? Hikers on smooth ground look ahead and scan the scenery. They naturally assume their feet are not going to stumble on every mouse dropping on the trail. They have confidence in their feet's built-in intelligence. If you are going to make short turns easily, you should, too.

Some instructors suggest that, in short turns on a smooth slope, you pick out a target at the end of the run--a prominent tree or a lift tower--and aim your run at that target so that your turn-radius for right and left turns is about the same and you make a conscious effort to keep them that way. Good idea. This tactic also forces you to take into account terrain changes and to regulate your speed and turn-shape accordingly. But try this targeting exercise only on smooth slopes. In bumps, even easy ones, concentrate on the bulls-eye for your next turn, not the turn you are making.

TIP NO. 13

Watch the girls go by

You don't have to stand on a corner to watch very interesting women go by. They are on many ski slopes and men, as well as other ladies, can learn a great deal by studying their style. As I've admitted before, some of the smoothest skiers I know are women in their 50s and 60s and a few in their 70s. What better excuse do you need to keep the ladies in view? You're watching them for educational purposes.

As a group, there are three things they do that makes their skiing look effortless. First, they are in charge of their skiing and ski gently as if they are ballroom dancing. Second, they are fussy about where they turn and pick only the places that suit them. And third, they slow down for possible trouble spots and proceed at a comfortable pace.

Obviously, they have to be good skiers to accomplish these maneuvers. Some of them wedge a little, but it doesn't show. Others are a bit tentative in using their poles. But when they ask for advice, I often tell them not to change anything--except to keep their head up and so everyone can see their smile.

TIP NO. 14

Read the terrain

A competent golfer wouldn't think of putting until he studied the undulations in a green. An experienced hiker always seeks the easiest route up a hill. Mountain bikers try to find the smoothest way down a rocky path. And skiers should try the find the flattest spot to turn on.

All ski slopes are not created equally steep. Everyone has little islands of flatness or at least places that are more level than the surrounding terrain. Check out the territory before entering. Is there an easy run-out in case you need it? Is the snow on one side of the trail less groomed than on the other side? Is there a way to arrive at your final destination without a long traverse or an uphill climb?

One of the most difficult tasks for an instructor is to get students in the habit of finding terrain that is skier friendly. "Wow," the pupils exclaims, "this is too steep!" The instructor replies, "OK, then follow me--stay right in my tracks--an we'll find an easier way down." But how does the instructor teach the student to read the terrain when the student isn't in class? It's basically the student's problem. And all he needs to do to solve it is to take the time to look down the hill and plan a strategy for the descent.

TIP NO. 15

The new rotation

If you learned to ski when you had a full head of hair and Elvis was alive and in Hollywood, you probably were taught the Arlberg Technique. There was nothing wrong with it at the time because most skis had the flexibility of axe handles and grooming was something the French did to poodles. Rotation was a major element of that technique and was done largely with the shoulders to force stiff skis through deep snow.

As you know, shoulders play a much less important role in turning now and their main function is to keep your parka from falling to your knees. But I'm trying to play this cozy--I don't want you to think that everything you learned previously is wrong. Shoulders, in fact your whole body, is used in skiing. But shoulders, and especially the way they were once employed, aren't the power tools they used to be.

Now the turning movement is performed with your lower body--hips, legs and feet. They swivel under your shoulders while your shoulders provide a relatively constant base for their movement. But--I'll deny it if you ever say I said it--when you are up to your belly button in heavy, wet snow or powder, use your downhill shoulder to grind your way around in the crud when no one is looking.

TIP NO. 16

Relax

Yes, I know I have emphasized many times the need to be relaxed in all types of skiing. But now your mind is as full of details as a Super Bowl commentary and you have forgotten to unwind. It's more important than ever because you can't possibly remember everything you should. And you don't need to.

That's the point. Modern ski technique consists of a series of building blocks. The first block forms the basis for learning in the second block, and so on until you reach your full potential. Hardly anything is discarded along the way. So when you get to, say, the seventh building block, you have had ample opportunity to practice fundamental movements over and over, and they can be performed as second nature.

Therefore, in the seventh block, you can concentrate on only what's new to you. At least that's the theory. In practice, you must occasionally review what you have learned and hone your technique. But you are still working on fewer refinements than you did in the third block. For example, Olympic-caliber skiers often make a conscious effort to ski on one ski at a time when they are practicing so that they can have a better feel or where their balance should be. Good recreational skiers often take a lesson, not to learn something new, but as a refresher.

CHAPTER V

Bumps

When I recently had the pleasure to ski with one of the patriarchs of modern ski technique, I asked him, then 72 years young and looking and skiing like 60, how he handled bumps. "I avoid them," he explained with a laugh. Of course, he still gets into moguls occasionally and he certainly knows how to handle them. But he doesn't make a practice of finding bumpy terrain. These days he is more concerned with his physical condition, especially his legs and back, and he plans to stay fit so he can ski comfortably in his 80s.

My friend has been on skis full time every winter since he served with the Army Ski Troops in World War II. He knows what his body can endure and isn't about to press his luck. Skiing has enough to offer him without the need of punishing his body. Frankly I, a little younger than my friend, haven't completely learned that lesson and I have paid the price. But I'm catching on. I don't avoid bumps, but I avoid too many bumps.

You may feel that bumps aren't your cup of tea and prefer to leave them for the young hot shots. But hold on for a minute. You can have fun in bumps if you take your time, ski slowly, and don't try to crash down every bump in a mogul field. You may not ever grow to love a bump but, like switching to decaffeinated coffee, you might eventually appreciate it more than the high-test stuff.

At your senior age, there are only three basic things you need to do to get through a mogul field. First, use your legs as shock absorbers--that is, extend your legs in troughs and bend your knees going over bumps. Second, ski as you do when making short turns with particular attention to being aggressive, staying forward, planting your poles, and looking on to your next targeted turning spot well before you get to it. And third, turn on only those bumps which look friendly (after you try this for a while, you may find that you can expand your circle of bump friends).

What you shouldn't do is to join a bump class with a group of young bashers unless you're into learning survival technique. Your body probably isn't ready for this and your delayed reaction time will make the experience frustrating. Learning to ski bumps should not be a pie-eating contest in which you cram in everything that's put before you. But you know that. You're older and have all the wisdom the world has to offer. Besides, you're not keeping score or trying to impress reckless youth.

In the standard bump lesson, students are often asked to follow their instructor in traversing a mogul field. It's a good exercise for you, too--if you do it slowly enough. The idea is to indicate how much leg flexion and extension is required while your head remains relatively steady in relation to general curvature of the hill. Visualize that your head is attached to a taut clothesline stretched across the slope and, when crossing this mogul field, your head isn't bobbing up and down because your legs extend in troughs and bend on bumps to keep your body stable.

Turning is done where it's the easiest--on the bump when the tip and tail of your skis are off the snow or in troughs if there are troughs on the downhill side of bumps. Obviously, this instruction is more effective on snow than in print. Excellent bump skiers say they "dive" into turns, but this term should be used advisedly. In deep bumps you do dive, then turn and slow down in a trough--preferably on the downhill side of the trough where the snow is softer because it has been scraped off the trough.. Experts sometimes even lean on their poles for balance. But if you can accomplish this, you're ready for a mogul competition.

Seniors should take it easy on themselves. Review how to make short turns and practice them on a smooth slope before venturing into moguls. Remember the importance of staying forward while standing on your whole foot, keeping your arms forward and planting your poles, and looking at your next turning place instead of at the turn you are in. Sitting back in bumps is courting disaster. You are probably going to wedge a little as you turn to slow down, but no one will notice as long as you remain upright.

TIP NO. 17

Moguls for everyone

In the ancient days before grooming, moguls grew almost as high as an elephant's eye. Falling off one could be a traumatic experience. But skiing in these minor mountains was comparatively easy if you weren't acrophobic because you could spend most of your time skiing in the valleys surrounding them. The only problem was that the cat-walks below these hills were often narrow and ski tips had a tendency to stick into the upper bank.

Now that skiing has gone high-tech with magnificent groomers and vastly improved boots, skis and binding, the skiing world is a much more satisfying place in which to live. Well, sort of. The bad news is that excellent grooming makes steeper terrain more accessible for rutting up and the new-design boots, skis and bindings foster mogul-making. The good news is that you wouldn't be able to ski today's moguls without the new equipment.

Moguls are now a fact of ski life. The good kind are round, soft and low. They can be fun but beware of the ones with deep valleys where rocks often lurk. The bad ones are hard, long and narrow, as if someone spilled a box of giant cigars across the hill. Caution is advised because they don't offer a decent platform on which to turn. And the worst ones are icy slivers that are best negotiated with ice skates.

Take your choice. Or don't take it--there's usually a smoother way to go around the worst of them. But get used to easy bumps. Moguls, like the common cold, aren't going away any time soon. But your comfort level in them may be increasing--sometimes.

TIP NO. 18

Know when to say no

Take a good look. Do you really want to ski down those bumps? All moguls aren't for everyone. Some moguls are the type you wish your mother-in-law would try. And other moguls are made for your talents. Honest. But frankly, I have yet to conduct a ski class when students wanted to ride bumps all day. Most often, a couple of hours is long enough, and sometimes too long.

Even with the best of grooming, every ski area is bound to have a few moguls. If they are easy ones and you have had your morning dosage of confidence vitamins, try them because they can be fun. Furthermore, you might as well get used to them because, like airline fares, there are always some new ones around.

However, if you want no part of moguls, just say no. But don't wait until you reach a trail where there is no way out of bumps. Check a trail map. The slopes and trails marked green and blue should be duck soup for intermediates. If you are in doubt, ask a ski patrolman or ski instructor which trail to take. If you mistakenly venture onto a black diamond, with or without bumps, that is beyond your comfort level, please take off your skis and walk down the side of the trail. You'll be doing yourself--and the ski patrol--a favor.

TIP NO. 19

Go back to basics

For ten years, I was a junior ice hockey coach in my spare time. The kids always wanted to try fancy stick handling and tricks that they saw the pros do on TV. But we always started our practice session by skating--forward, backward, cross-overs, relays, stop and start, circles, and fall down and get up. I was drilling them in the basics. They couldn't achieve their potential unless they could skate well, and I wanted them to be as good as possible so they would want to stay in the sport.

Unfortunately, I don't have the same rein on my ski school students. I can only suggest that they return to the basics when they think their skiing needs help, or to reaffirm that what they are doing is OK. Perhaps you think I'm over-doing this bit because I've said it so often. But my argument is that, if this idea is good enough for Olympic competitors--and it is--then it should also be worthwhile for recreational skiers.

Which basics you get back to are up to you. Everyone--everyone!--has an off day occasionally, and for a variety of personal reasons. Sometimes you are tired, mentally unprepared, or just can't get into skiing. If you are too far out of it, maybe you should hang up your skis for a day and get yourself together. But before you do, try executing a few fundamental maneuvers to get yourself back on track. It can work better than aspirin.

CHAPTER VI

Powder

There are more misconceptions about skiing powder than about any other experience in the sport. The term "powder" itself is misleading. There's feather-light powder and heavy powder, shallow powder and deep powder, and yahoo powder that you wallow in. Realizing this confusion, you might think that you can't ski powder. You can. Perhaps you've heard that you sit back to ski powder. You don't. Maybe you feel your skis are not soft enough or wide enough to handle powder. They are OK in most conditions.

In general, you ski powder the same way you ski groomed snow. That's an over-simplification for very heavy or deep powder but it's a good place to start. If you are skiing in powder that's only boot-top high and has poor moisture content for making snowballs, you actually do ski the way you normally would. If the powder is just below your knees, you should make a few changes--feet a little closer together, more bend in your knees when you finish a turn, almost equal weight on each ski but with the downhill ski still supporting slightly more weight than the uphill ski, and pole plants that are firm but not frog-stickers.

Time out. When I show these first two paragraphs to my powder skiing experts, they suggested three strategies that need to be emphasized before a skier gets into the nitty-gritty of skiing powder, particularly deep powder. First, you must ski faster than you normally do to stay afloat in powder. Second, you should point your skis down the hill and stay in the fall-line longer than you normally would in order to attain the speed which is necessary to overcome the resistance of deep snow. And third, once you get up your nerve and do this, visualize yourself skiing in slow motion because the heavy snow delays your turning movements and forces you to wait until your skis finally change direction.

This means that a powder skier is in a major balancing act, the earthy equivalent of a tight-rope walker in a circus. Are you ready for this experience? Let's proceed.

In knee-deep powder your biggest problem is in generating enough power to initiate turns. The deep snow holds you back and you need more energy--and more speed-- to get your skis moving into the fall line. Start by traversing across the slope. Your feet are closer together and almost equally weighted to provide a solid platform. Your knees are flexed and your weight is properly distributed because you have just planted your downhill pole to put your body in readiness to turn. Now there's just one more thing to do to turn. Rise to stand tall and, at the same time, start twisting your feet into the turn as you would on a packed slope. But rise quickly and make a little hop by raising the tails of your skis as you turn.

This hop is as big as you need to get the tips of your skis started pointing toward the fall line. It's more of a swing with your lower body doing the swinging. Some skiers get into it with a slight wedge. You still accelerate in the turn and this increased speed and foot twist carry you into the traverse to set you up for the next turn the opposite way. Powder turns are basically long turns that you control on a shorter radius so that you don't pick up too much speed. Try a turn and stop. Try again without stopping and move into your next turn.

Controlling speed is the essence of powder skiing. To stay in control, you must turn. And starting your turn--not turning which is easy due to the increased resistance from the deep snow--requires aggressive effort. If you lose too much speed, you flounder because turning becomes more difficult. If you gain too much speed, your skis tend to plane to the top of the snow, you lose your confidence, sit back, and then it's adios, amigo.

Even when you get the hang of it, powder skiing is hard work. Expect to sweat and be sucking for breath when you reach the bottom of the hill. It's the rhythm of lazy turn after lazy turn--which look lazy but actually require a lot of effort--that make powder skiing exciting. And you are still using the same basic technique that you employed to graduate from the bunny hill.

A word about equipment. You don't need extremely tight boots to ski well in deep powder--just tight enough so that your heel doesn't rise. If you plan to get into deep-powder skiing, those fat-stick powder skis work great--if you have mastered the basic technique of skiing powder. Of course, you'll need to wear water-resistant or water-proof ski clothing unless you can stand freezing your knees and buns in jeans.

TIP NO. 20

Ski in a storm

A student once asked, "Do the ski lifts operate in a snow storm?" The pupil was a beginner, of course, and didn't realize that, if visibility is adequate, skiing in fresh snow is one of the joys of the sport. But even intermediate skiers are wary of storms. It all depends on how ferocious the storm is. If it appears that you will be physically uncomfortable, stay indoors. But if the snow is the Christmas card type, give it a whirl.

High winds are no fun. Wet, sticky snow that sticks to your goggles isn't worth the effort. And snow mixed with rain should be left for polar bears. But gently falling, dry snow brings out real skiers who call in sick and head for the hills to take advantage of the excellent skiing it offers. You, too, should go for it. But go equipped with a hat, goggles, and a scarf or neck gator if there's a chance for a storm. Dress in layers to be prepared for the worst. It also helps to get your skis waxed.

TIP NO. 21

Be an old smoothie

    Skiing in powder is like dancing the waltz. The people who waltz best are in a seemingly effortless rhythm of turns. For skiers, a similar turn and glide is repeated in what appear to be lazy turns down the hill. But in skiing as in waltzing, movements only look like they are performed easily. Dancers require practice to keep their feet untangled. Skiers need to put some zap into getting their turns started.

    Nowhere in skiing is rhythm more important than in powder--not only to appear as if you are floating comfortably but to stay in balance so there will be a next turn. So, as usual, start on a gentle slope you know you can handle, but one on which you can accelerate when you turn. What you definitely do not want to do is to jack your turn around with a jerky movement. If you need a narrow wedge to start turning, then wedge with the expectation that you'll eventually find the balance you need for parallel turns. To achieve that, never stay in the wedge very long. Be parallel before you reach the fall line.

    Only with parallel skis can you really float through powder the way they do in the ski movies. Otherwise, you fight the increased pressure of deep snow and your balance isn't supported almost equally by both skis. And, please, don't move on to steep terrain until you feel at ease on gentle slopes. Skiing powder takes extra effort. You want to avoid getting bushed by righting yourself after falls on slopes that are over your head.

CHAPTER VII

Ice, Heavy Wet Snow and Other Bad Stuff

Bad Stuff requires caution. Now think about it--what should you do to be cautious? You put your feet a little farther apart because feel you need better balance. You stand more straight up, partly because you don't relish taking a header but mainly because you need to use your whole ski--tips and tails--to prevent catastrophe. You keep your weight more evenly distributed on both feet and never lean into the hill. And you try to relax even though your inclination is to stiffen up.

Ice: You do all these things, of course. But you also check your skis to make sure you have reasonably sharp edges (if you don't know what reasonably sharp edges are, get your education at a ski shop). Turning is a snap on ice. The hard part is completing a turn without sliding sideways. You are definitely going to skid sideways--everyone does. So use your edges. Crank your knees into the hill as soon as you cross the fall line to put both skis on edge. Or, if you are on glare ice, actually jump on the edge of your down hill ski to carve a line in the ice. Jam it hard, then get back on the edges of both skis. You may wedge momentarily as you cross the fall line. But so what--hopefully, you are still standing, something that not many skiers on ice can say.

Heavy wet snow: If it's too heavy and wet, go to a movie. But if you think you can mush through it, use the standard lousy-condition movements noted above--with two major exceptions. Skip the edging bit entirely. And turn as you would in powder--wedge into the fall line or hop the tails of both skis up and out so that the tips are pointed more nearly down the fall line, then grind your way through the rest of the turn as you would normally with hands in front and your hair standing on end. Don't forget the pole plant before you hop.

Rocks: If you are skiing among rocks, you are probably skiing among moguls. So use your bump technique--especially, when you are in a turn to avoid rocks, rely on your feet to remember to complete the turn and immediately set your mind on where you next turn will be. If you can't avoid skiing over rocks, don't panic--and don't sit back because you have too much invested in your ski pants, underwear and skin if you fall.

Heavy fog or fiercely blowing snow: Take the lift down and look for three other skiers to play bridge with.

Extreme cold: Keep moving all body parts. Wiggle your toes, fingers and ears. Buckle your boots a little looser. Cover your head and ears. Wear mittens instead of gloves. Wear goggles. If you are skiing a big mountain, go in for hot chocolate after every run. Do not wear tight clothing or so many clothes that blood circulation is restricted. Don't put on an extra pair of heavy socks that will cramp your feet, but do wear under-layer socks of man-made material that will wick away moisture from your feet Avoid alcohol until the end of the day when you can accept congratulations for surviving.

Crud: This is deep and heavy snow that has been cut up by other skiers. Nobody skis it smoothly--join the ragged crowd. See "Heavy wet snow." Good luck.

Crust: There are two kinds, unbreakable and breakable. For unbreakable, ski it as you would a groomed slope and use your edges. For breakable, enjoy it as a new life experience or, for even more fun, go have a root canal operation.

Death cookies: These are chunks of ice that are infrequently churned up at night by grooming machines working under changing climatic conditions. They are not fun. See "root canal" above.

Spring skiing: This is definitely not "bad stuff" unless the snow is heavy and wet. Spring is the time for corn snow--pellets of ice the size of aspirin tablets--which makes skiing feel like riding on ball bearings. This is a good feeling and should not give you a headache. Furthermore (in the Believe Or Not category), skiing on corn snow in light rain is a wonderful experience providing you stay dry (a plastic garbage-can liner helps). Besides dark glasses and plenty of suntan cream, you need to layer clothing with a light, wind-proof and water-proof parka on the outside and a sweater, which can be easily removed, on the inside. Wear a fanny pack for storing a discarded sweater, sun cream and other essentials.

TIP NO. 22

Play it smart

You are obviously blessed with supreme sagacity because you have decided that skiing is for you. Don't spoil the romance. If the weather and snow conditions look dangerous, bag it and go bowling (watch out for lurking indoor germ cultures and be careful that you don't strain yourself with that heavy ball).

But wait a minute. Are the storm and wind abating? Was that a sliver of a sunbeam that pierced that cloud? Perhaps you should linger awhile and check out conditions after fortifying yourself with hot chocolate. Skiing is often wonderful immediately following a storm. And even when snow conditions do not appear to be particularly inviting, they are usually better on some parts of the mountain than on others. The trick is to use the great wisdom you possess to locate the nice parts.

For example, the amount of snow that falls in a storm is often greater and drier on the top of a big mountain than it is on the lower slopes. When the snow base is hard, seek out slopes that face the sun where the snow softens earlier. Conversely, fluffy snow on sun slopes turns to mashed potatoes. For safety's sake, don't ski alone; locate ski patrol phones by reading a trail map. And when snow conditions are iffy, use trails which have a run-out at the bottom.

In short, use your head when deciding when and where you should ski. Trust your intelligence to know the difference between accepting an exciting challenge and courting disaster. Bowling can be fun, but rising above your expectations in skiing is jubilation.

TIP NO. 23

Go for the groomed

Practice may not make perfection but it certainly assists improvement. It can also be a pain in the back. I know. A few years back, I was obsessed with the desire to improve my performance in bumps. I stayed in the bumps too long and, as a result, I spent too much time in a hot tub easing the ache in my back. If I had been smarter, I could have practiced quick turns on groomed slopes and then only occasionally returned to the moguls to hone my technique.

Seniors and grandparents don't need to punish themselves to become well-rounded skiers. When you have the opportunity, ski a little powder--or crud or wet, heavy stuff--on the edges of groomed trails. On easy terrain, cut through the trees between trails for a short distance to get the feel of what unpacked snow is like, and to learn what you can and cannot do in it. A good way to experience new conditions is to find those slopes that were groomed before a storm ended and still have some fluffy snow on them.

But before and after experimentation, do on groomed slopes what you hoped to do in more difficult conditions. Try to develop a mindset--if I can do it on manicured terrain, I can do it anyplace. With a little courage, you can. And you will--if you have full confidence when the skiing is easy.

CHAPTER VIII

Equipment

Ah hah, you say. We've finally reached a subject in skiing where I can express my special individuality, where I can be Me and not just one of the blobs in the huddled masses, and where my innate uniqueness will stand out in a crowd. The Me Generation lives--long live the Me Generation!

Back off. I've been preaching for seven chapters and 23 Tips that, although there are essential elements that must be learned--like respecting the power of gravity--skiing is an individual sport which must be flavored with each skier's innate uniqueness. That is, what works best for you is the way to go. However, while you may bend the fundamentals of skiing technique, you can't break them.

The same is true of equipment and clothing, in skiing as in any activity. I've suggested that renting equipment is a good way check out equipment for clues as to what you might want to buy. Golfers and tennis players demo clubs and racquets before finalizing a purchase. They want to make sure they get equipment that feels right before investing. People kicking tires on cars have a similar decision to make--lease or purchase. It depends on what they can afford and how long they intend to keep a vehicle. Think of getting skiing paraphernalia--which is not inexpensive--with the same thought process.

In short, ski equipment, like ski technique, must work for you. Don't let a sales clerk con you into buying something because it is "very fashionable" or "our best seller" or is endorsed by a ski-racing champion. Those are valid considerations for purchasing but they should not be the primary reasons.

A. Boots

As real estate salesmen say, the three main considerations in buying property are location, location and location. In purchasing ski boots, the three main considerations are fit, fit and fit. Buy a ski boot just as you would any shoe. Pick a store that knows shoes and has a good selection. Try several brands. Walk around in them. Change the adjustments. Walk some more. How do they feel? How does the price feel? What is the store's refund policy? Should you try another store before you make a decision?

This is essential--try on boots while wearing the socks you plan to ski in and make sure there's enough room for expansion of your feet when they get warm. Also, never buy a boot in which your toes butt against the toe of the boot, or a boot that you hope you can fill with extra socks. When being fitted and when skiing, wear a thin liner sock and a medium-weight or heavy sock (never cotton) that fits your foot closely (not the one-size-fits-all type). The liner sock, of man-made material, serves two purposes--it transfers perspiration to the heavier sock where it can evaporate more easily, and it provides a slick surface to allow the heavier sock, which retains heat from your foot, to move as is needed fill up your boot.

In the early 1970s, some of the then-new buckle boots were made of heavy and nearly inflexible man-made material. They were warm and needed only a liner sock. And they served well if the fit was good--in fact, world-class downhill competitors used this type of boot for a number of years. However, they weren't popular with recreational skiers and manufacturers went to more flexible materials that didn't hold heat as well. As a result, many skiers resorted to heavy hiking socks to keep their feet warm. With further technical advances, today's boots keep feet warm when only medium-weight outer socks are used. In addition, several styles of battery-operated foot warmers and boots with extra insulation are available to keep feet toasty.

Modern boots employ a variety of contraptions to keep feet tightly in boots. These devices also have adjustments to provide comfort. Every boot has a system to keep your heel from rising when skiing and to make it relatively easy to get in and out of. Some boots have gadgets that control the stiffness or the amount of forward lean that is permitted in the ankle. Some allow widening of the boot at the ball of the foot. I particularly like this widening feature because it allows me flexibility as my foot swells or the boot heats up and expands.

Much has been said about the virtues of boots that buckle down the front as opposed to rear-entry boots that, as the name indicates, flop open in back for entry and exit and require fewer buckles for closure. Frankly, I don't see much difference between them as long as the fit is proper. From force of habit, I use the buckle type when I plan to spend a lot of time riding serious bumps and making quick turns.

Recreational skiers, especially seniors, don't need all the bells and whistles on sophisticated racing boots. And they don't need the top-of-the-line high price either. But they should get those amenities that can make them ski better with maximum comfort. You need to adjust your boots several times a day--at the top of the hill for your first run, at and after lunch, and when relaxing at the end of the day--and you should buy boots which permit adjustments. Come to think of it, why don't they make cigarette lighters in cars optional so non-smokers can save a buck?

If you are knock-kneed or bow-legged, you will need an adjustment for the cant of your feet--that is, the tilt to the inside or outside. In fact, many people need canting of one or both feet to make skis flat on the snow for straight running and for the proper angle in turns. Canting is done two ways--by placing wedges under ski-boot insoles as is done in the better rental shops; or by a mechanism built into more expensive ski boots. The possible need for canting is another reason why a reputable ski shop is your best bet for the purchase of ski equipment.

To avoid pitfalls when walking in ski boots, buckle all the buckles, even if only lightly, so that buckles don't catch on something that could trip you. Lodges, parking lots and buses are uncomfortable places for a sitzmark.

B. Skis and bindings

Skis are like the tires on your car--they are under you for safe and comfortable travel and, if you buy them from a reputable dealer and pay enough (but not too much) for them, they will serve you well. In other words, finding a serviceable, reasonably-priced pair of skis these days is no sweat. They won't twist or fall apart and you may even be able to find them in colors to complement your new parka, boots, and old school ring.

But unlike tires, skis react differently under people who are short or tall, skinny or rotund, wimps or weight lifters, long legged or short legged--even men or women. A person's sense of balance, aggressiveness and athletic ability are also important considerations in selecting skis. Identical twins often prefer dissimilar ski lengths and flexes. The trick is to select the skis that are just right for you and your dealer can help a great deal.

Renting skis is a snap if you are a beginner. Simply tell the sports shop clerk how many days you have skied and he will give you the length you require. Rental skies for novices are pretty much the same. Starting out, they will be about chest high. For each step you progress in the first few lessons, swap them for skis 10 centimeters longer each time. But don't push it--too short skis are better than too long skis when you are entering the sport. Novices should rent until they learn what length they are comfortable on.

If you are buying skis, rely on the sports-shop expert to select the length. He can probably pick a length that is within 5 centimeters of being correct for you--if in doubt, go shorter rather than longer. Now comes the hard part--choosing the flex that you will enjoy the most. Most seniors will appreciate a relatively soft flex, especially if they plan to ski mostly in the soft snow of the Rocky Mountains. If they ski in the more compact snow in the East or Midwest, or the wetter snow on the Pacific Coast, a bit stiffer flex may be in order. The only way you can learn which of the many brands, lengths and flexes you will like most is to try out a couple of different makes. Ask to rent a pair of demonstration skis.

A ski of the correct length with a relatively soft flex (that means a flex that is not very hard or very soft) is your all-season tire. It will work well in powder, hard snow, wet snow, crud and on groomed slopes. There are specialty skis for very deep powder and stiff skis for ice but you won't need them unless you intend to take up residence in a ski resort. Even if you do move to a ski resort, you do not need to purchase new skis every year. Skis made today are built to last--and to be used.

You may be surprised to read that I have never found the perfect pair of skis for all snow conditions. But you shouldn't be. That ski has never been built and never will be. I currently have nine pair of skis in my arsenal ranging from less than a year to 20 years old and from 190 to 204 centimeters long. Most have a relatively soft or relaxed flex although the flex is different for each pair--some have soft tips and stiff tails, and vice versa, and some have an even flex the full length of the ski. But on the type of snow for which I use each pair, the "feel" of all these skis is quite similar. I have my favorites but I ski on most of them every winter (several are kept in the storage room for nostalgic reasons).

Now you are thinking that if I can't make up my mind, how should I expect you to decide what's best for you? Answer: check with your good buddy at your favorite ski shop. That's my point--he has at least a dozen pair of skis that are just your ticket.

Bindings: Selection here is easy, even though there is a surfeit of offerings. All popular brands do a good job of holding your boot on your ski and releasing your boot when you fall. Some have unique features that require a complete sales pitch to understand. Don't buy the least expensive--your safety is worth more than they cost. And you probably don't require the expensive bindings that racers need (the metal springs in these bindings may be too strong for your type of recreational skiing because they are designed to release in hard crashes). Stick with the middle of the price range. Choose a color that matches your skis (or don't if you feel funky).

C. Poles

You're in luck. You've finally found something in skiing that is fairly inexpensive--if you can live with a shade less glitz. Ski poles should be light and strong, have a comfortable grip, and be the proper length. All but the very cheapest are serviceable enough, grip comfortably, and come in your size (or can be cut down to the length you need). Proper length is easy to ascertain. Simply place the pole upside down on the floor, grab the pole below the basket, and if your arm is parallel to the floor, this is the pole for you.

In general, the major difference in poles is in what some pole makers call "balance" which, loosely translated, means how much they weigh. Less weight requires more expensive materials and, therefore, poles are priced in inverse proportion to their weight. If you can easily handle a few grams more weight--and you certainly can--then the pole you need will cost considerably less than the one designed for NASA space walkers. What a deal.

D. Clothing

This is a short discourse on function, not fashion, because I'm more concerned with comfort than being chic (my wife suggested that I put an exclamation point after that sentence). If ski garb doesn't promise to keep me warm and dry, I'm not interested in it (my wife insists that I favor anything with yard-sale pricing). I admit to a tendency to retain ski outfits that may be slightly faded and well past their prime, but that's because I'm a recycler at heart and often find use of warm-up pants and wind shirts for hiking, camping, fishing, and washing the car (my wife says I gloat in being cheap).

At the risk of being risqué, I'll tell you what I wear from the inside out on a sunny winter day with the temperature in the mid-20s F. Bottom: medium-weight long johns over my regular briefs--never cotton long johns because cotton absorbs perspiration and makes my legs cold, and never wool next to my skin because I'm one of those strange people that wool itches (think of the problems I had as a swab-jockey in the Navy).

Top: long-sleeve T-shirt of man-made material under a loose, heavy cotton flannel shirt, then a light nylon wind shirt (they're hard to get now except at yard sales), a medium-weight or heavy wool sweater (depending on the weather) with buttons or a zipper at the throat, and a wind and moisture-resistant parka with a high collar on the outside. I use the inner wind shirt for two reasons--it seems to keep me warmer but, most important, it has a slippery surface that allows my sweater to slip around rather than binding when I move my arms.

I know I'm breaking ski-instructor tradition by wearing a loose-fitting cotton lumberman's shirt instead of a cotton T-neck. But the T-neck doesn't work for me because it absorbs perspiration that makes me feel clammy. My parka isn't made of that wonderful stuff that breaths because I haven't found that the extra cost is worth the breathing feature. But it very well may be just what you need. If someone gave me a parka made of this material, I'd gladly accept it--as I do when I am annually issued a ski-instructor's parka that breaths.

Bottom, outside: I've left this for last because I have trouble here. Being a senior, my waistline seems to add or subtract an inch or so on its own whim (maybe the thickness of my lumberman's shirt has something to do with it) and I don't like to be bound-up around the middle when I bend over or sit down. So I prefer loose-fitting insulated, warm-up type ski pants held up by suspenders. When I'm wearing a light shirt, regular stretch ski pants work fine, but only the over-the-boot style, never the in-the-boot type that collect snow in the boot or require the use of a gator to keep out snow.

Hats: they say that your head serves as the radiator for your body. I like my radiator warm so I wear a wool hat with man-made material in the brow to prevent itching, or a felt-type wool hat with ear flaps and a sweat band.

Hand covering: Take your choice--gloves or mittens. Insulation in gloves has come a long way in providing increased comfort. But when, baby, it's cold outside, I bring out the mittens with glove liners.

Other warmers: there are a number of styles of face masks if you need one, and some people do. Scarfs are fine but don't let them dangle outside where they can get caught in chairlifts or branches you pass by. Those fuzzy neck gators serve better to keep you cozy. I couldn't ski in cold weather without having my ears covered. And you definitely need to wear sun glasses or goggles--for warmth as well as eye protection. In fact, in very cold weather or windy conditions, I use goggles to cover my face.

TIP NO. 24

A good ski shop is a skier's best friend

Most of what I've learned about ski equipment I've learned from professionals who operate specialty ski shops. There weren't many of these shops around when I finally earned enough money to move up from the army surplus skis, boots, poles and even clothing I had acquired to get into the sport. Then skiing came on strong and the number of specialty shops grew by taking on sidelines to keep busy in the spring, summer and fall. Except at ski resorts, selling skis is often a sideline itself in large stores that cover the sporting goods waterfront from archery to water polo.

But there are knowledgeable people around who can be of great assistance in helping skiers people with their individual needs. As I have mentioned, ski equipment manufacturers are now doing a good job in training sales clerks who sell their gear. The department-type stores that handle ski goods often offer amazingly-low prices on excellent merchandise, but you have to know what you need specifically to take advantage of the discounts.

The only way to find out if a ski store knows its beans is to ask questions that clerks should be able to answer. I did that once in a large metropolitan outlet. Answering my question of whether the store carried skins for going uphill on cross-country skis, the clerk said, "Oh, they don't make those anymore." I knew differently--they not only make them but they make them in assorted colors, sizes and materials. I hope this book gives you the ammunition you need to make meaningful inquiries.

TIP NO. 25

Look good in the bar

Let's assume you have just finished a day of skiing while on vacation at a major ski resort, have taken a shower, and are now wondering what to wear for après-skiing. Answer: anything. Really, anything. I pose the question because ski school students ask me that. They are usually the people who come to a resort with trunks full of clothing they will never use. Besides all your ski gear, you should only need enough other stuff for a week's vacation to fill one suitcase and one carry-on bag.

Ski resorts are very democratic places. Except in fancy hotels (and sometimes not even there), there are no dress codes as in some places in Europe. But North American skiers do dress up if only in a colorful shirt and jeans covered by the parka they wore skiing. Western hats are popular, at least in the West.

TIP NO. 26

Wonderful wool

My mother was a champion knitter and I still have a cable knit sweater and three cardigans she made when she learned that her little boy was going to take up skiing seriously. They still keep me warm and I think of her every time I wear them. You just can't beat wool for warmth and wear ability. That's the trouble--I can't wear them out and I refuse to give any of them to the Thrift Shop.

Although you may not be able to beat wool, you can tie it with some of the fuzzy man-made materials available today. Sweaters and jackets of this type are not only warm and serviceable; some brands are actually wind-proof. What's more they don't retain moisture the way wool does, they can be washed with other clothes, most stains clean up easily, and they come in all sorts of color-fast hues.

What's a man to do--revere the past or salute the present? I figure that mother knows best, even if she didn't know about the new miracle fabrics. I still wear her sweaters--but not as much as I used to.

TIP NO. 27

Layer for comfort

It was invented by Neanderthal Woman ("Thor, remember to take an extra deerskin on your hunting trip in case you get chilled"). Golfers, hikers and skiers have used it for years but they didn't have a name for it. Ski manufacturers have now adopted the concept and the terminology. Layering is simply dressing for skiing so that you have at least one article of clothing to shed if you're hot or put on when you're cold.

In its simplest form it means wearing a warm sweater under a shell parka or anorak (one of which can be taken off, depending on the weather) instead of a heavy parka that might provide a personal steam bath when you sweat. Layering is particularly suited to spring skiing but it works in cold months because manufacturers have developed roomy, water-resistant, wind-proof, and fashionable jackets that give comfort without a surfeit of padding. Of course, at times during a ski season, there is good reason to bundle up in a cozy down parka. But on many days you do not need to be a clone of Admiral Byrd in expedition garb trudging onward to the North Pole.

If you layer, you may want to wear a fanny pack or light backpack to carry extra or discarded clothes. You don't need a pack if you don't mind a bulge in your jacket made by an extra sweater tied around your waist. Layering sure beats leaving unneeded clothing at the top or bottom of lifts and then not having it handy when clouds and cold winds blow in.

CHAPTER IX

Cross-country Skiing

I'll admit that I'm almost as hooked on cross-country skiing as I am on alpine skiing--some days, more so. The two sports combine all the same elements--getting out in the fresh winter air, great natural scenery, sense of accomplishment in learning what to do and doing it well, and gliding along with a sense of rhythm with cooling air in your face. But XC skiing provides better exercise, and you can langlauf in almost all adverse weather. After hours of staring at a word-processor screen to write a tome like this, it's relaxing to take a jaunt around the golf course on skinny skis.

In Tip No. 4, "Cross-country sets the style," I noted that skiing cross-country enhances the balance which alpine skiers need. I also told how to do it--by moving your arms and legs the same way you would in hiking, by wedging in a V to slow down or stop, and by using an inverted V, or herringbone step, to get up inclines. That's the easy technical part.

Actually, that's about all beginning cross-country skiers need to know. Of course, when you wedge to slow down or reverse wedge to herringbone, you press your knees closer together to allow the edges of your skis to grip the snow better. When you side-step up a hill, you press your knees up-hill for the same reason. You hold XC poles the way you grip alpine poles--put your hands up through the loop before you grasp the handle. And you go as fast as you want easily, without waiting for a downhill slope to propel you.

It's probably called cross-country skiing because the Scandinavians who invented it skied across the countryside. Today, a more appropriate term is cross-golf-course skiing or through-the-woods skiing or around-the-park skiing, because that's how it's often employed. Henry Thoreau would have loved around-the-pond skiing.

A few words about costs and equipment. First of all, you don't need a lift ticket unless you try one of the excellent ski touring centers that have an extensive, groomed trail system (they are truly worth the small admission price). XC equipment is not inexpensive but it's considerably less than half the cost of alpine skis, boot, poles and bindings. Also, it's often easy to find good starter equipment in ski swaps, newspaper classified ads and end-of-season sales.

Boots: all of the newer styles cover your ankle to keep out snow. However, you'll need gators to wrap around your lower legs if you have to break trail in deep snow.

Bindings: boots and bindings are often sold as a package and work well together. Some are the step-in variety in which you push a lever only to step out.

My personal preference, because I break trail several times a month and occasionally try telemarking, are the old-style bear traps with a cable that goes behind the heel. Poles: cheap ones that are shoulder high are all you need. Skis: get skis with metal edges to make it easier to herringbone up hills and wedge going down hills. And unless you plan to take a graduate course in waxing, no-wax skis will serve adequately in all but a few snow conditions.

Clothing: anything goes unless you insist on emulating an Olympic racer and can pay Olympic prices. But remember that you are going to work up some body heat. The old adage about hiking applies to XC skiing--start cold and you'll get warm. Do not wear your expedition-weight downhill parka. Instead, layer your outer clothing with a sweater under a water-resistant shell. Lined work gloves are more comfortable than heavy alpine ski gloves and mittens. Definitely wear sun cream and a hat for both warmth and sun protection.

As with alpine skiing, a good ski shop is an XC skier's best friend. If you like to dance, you'll love cross-country waltzing on snow. You'll be happy to find that aren't too many dancers crowding the floor.

TIP NO. 28
Telemarking is worth the effort

Of course you know what a telemark is. It's the one-foot-advanced turn that ancient Scandinavians in bearskin clothes are making in historical drawings. And it hasn't changed much over the centuries. Perhaps you've seen movies of modern telemarkers with the knee of their trailing foot bent so far that it nearly touches that ski. If you did, you may have thought, "No thank you--that's for 20-year old triathletes."

You're partially correct. Telemarking does require considerable effort and agility. But if I can do it (and I try), you can too. But my feet are only a foot or 18 inches apart and both knees are slightly bent. In making a left turn, I lead with my right foot, put 60 percent of my weight on it, and twist it to the left. When I turn to near traversing the hill, I switch feet and turn the other way, scissoring my feet in each turn as I descend the slope.

The tricky part is maintaining your balance while you are scissoring and not chickening out by sitting back or leaning into the hill as the slope gets steeper. If you are skiing in a few inches of fluff on a solid snow base, the maneuver is a snap. But if the snow is heavy or deep, considerably more muscle and balance is required.

Telemarking in easy snow can be done on any kind of cross-country skis, but is most successfully performed on slightly wider touring skis (the metal-sandwich type) with steel edges. If you plan to try telemarking at a ski area, you'll need some kind of harness to keep the ski attached to your boot in case the binding releases. If you seek privacy for your maiden voyage, you will find that trudging up a hill is just as tough and tiring as going down. But it's fun.

TIP NO. 29

Ski to a mountain hut

This is the super-fun part of cross-country skiing and there are now huts available in many parts of the United States and Canada for this experience. How do I know? In central Colorado where we live, my wife and I lead overnight hut trips for 20 seniors once a month during the skiing season, and hiking trips from the huts once a month during the summer and early fall.

In Colorado alone, well over 20,000 nightly hut reservations are made by cross-country skiers at private and public facilities. State departments of tourism can provide information on where huts are located. Resort associations and chambers of commerce at ski areas also can answer questions about local hut systems and guide services.

Hut skiers must be in good physical condition because huts are usually located 3 to 8 miles from trailheads. In Colorado, most huts are in the high country which means you have ascents and descents--with a pack on your back. But, normally, you only have to carry food, sleeping bag and personal items (tooth brush, etc.) because the huts are often furnished with stoves for cooking and heating, wood for burning, and all necessary cooking and eating utensils. Some even have solar electrical lighting and propane stoves.

CHAPTER X

Miscellaneous and Everything Else

Why no illustrations in this text? Two reasons: first, because they are sometimes confusing since there is no perfect skiing form for every physical shape and ability any more than there is a perfect golf swing for everyone; and second, because if you try new movements on a super-gentle slope, you'll get the idea of what you want to accomplish without a how-to road map.

Did the author have helping hands? I take full responsibility for everything in this book, but the entire text was checked with fully certified professional instructors, internationally ranked racers, extreme skiers featured in widely distributed movies, and a former trainer for a national ski team. In each case, I specified that this book is intended for senior skiers and grandparents.

Should I retire to a major ski resort? Sure, if you really want to ski several days a week and, most important, if you can afford the pricey residences that are available at major resorts. Otherwise, the cost of living isn't too far out of line and there are good bargains in top-of-the-line ski equipment. But as the old saying goes, "you come for winter and stay for summer" when there are lots of warm weather activities. Caution: if you are thinking of moving to a ski resort because your life is a mess where you are, get your head straightened out where you are because there are too many diversions at ski resorts that interfere with the straightening process. Also, set aside some money that allows you to travel to the desert or ocean after a long ski season.

Should I join a ski club? Definitely. Most skiers are gregarious and fun to be with. And ski clubs, especially the ones for senior skiers, have ski travel programs that can introduce you to new areas and save you money on group rates.

How is the skiing in Europe? Just like skiing in the States or Canada--when the conditions are good, the skiing is great. I can personally vouch for superb resorts in Austria and Switzerland. But the information on trails and ski terrain is not as complete as it is here. Make sure you know where you are going to ski before you board a lift. However, you'll have trouble finding a poor restaurant on the slopes or in villages in Europe. Also, the scenery is spectacular.

Is this book for men AND women? You bet. I've emphasized ad nauseam the modern technique takes into account different physical shapes and talents. That means the different body configurations and athletic ability of men AND women. True, short people make slightly different movements than tall people, and stocky skiers turn with a little different motion than skinny skiers. Some women may not express the skiing bravado of some men. But they all use the same basic movements to turn, glide and stop. In fact, skiing should be considered a true unisex sport.

Can people with bum knees ski? Of course. I'm living proof. My right knee tells me when it is tired during the third set of tennis or after carrying a 30-pound pack five miles to a wilderness camp site. Then my orthopedic specialist, a U.S. Ski Team doctor, fitted me with a brace which works fine and makes me look quite macho in the ski instructors' locker room. Actually, a drug-store neoprene sleeve which kept my knee warm served adequately until recently. Ask your doctor what happens to knees in older people, and what can be done to correct the aging process. Modern medical science is amazing. There aren't many seniors who can use bad knees as their only excuse for not going skiing.

What are the author's credentials? If variety is the spice of life, I am spicy. In my former life, I was an ice hockey and baseball player in college (philosophy and religion major), 70s golfer who is lucky to break 90 now, an advertising manager for General Electric, editor of the Aspen Times newspaper, newspaper columnist, daily radio commentator, the Aspen Skiing Company's first marketing VP, 8-year county commissioner, and in my spare time, a junior baseball and hockey coach and a participant in about four-dozen community service organizations.

I've also skied a little--in grade school on pine skis with homemade bindings made from inner tubes, dodging trees in the Middlesex Fells way north of Boston; earned my C classification as a racer at Mad River Glen in Vermont; and raised and played transportation coordinator for four children, two boys and two girls, who occasionally give me ski lessons. Both girls have coached at ski academies and raced professionally and one was national champion and a member of U.S. Teams in the Olympics and World Championships. Both boys competed in national championships and one represented the U.S. in the Junior World Championships and makes part of his living jumping off cliffs for ski movies. At present, I am a writer and a retired ski instructor and have completed 53 years of residency in Aspen where my wife and I maintain a home base for tennis, camping, hiking, kayaking, fishing, mountain biking and other normal retirement pastimes. If you add up those years, although some of these endeavors overlap, you'll see that I'm only 86.

Copyright © 2013 by George Madsen. 124363-MADS

ISBN: Softcover   978-1-4797-9073-9
        Ebook   978-1-4797-9074-6

All rights reserved. No part of this book may be reproduced or transmitted in any form or by any means, electronic or mechanical, including photocopying, recording, or by any information storage and retrieval system, without permission in writing from the copyright owner.

To order additional copies of this book, contact:
Xlibris Corporation
1-888-795-4274
www.Xlibris.com
Orders@Xlibris.com

Printed in Great Britain
by Amazon